KID'S PARTY CHARACTERS

How to Be Financially Independent

Bringing JOY to Children

Written by Cheryl Jacobs, Author of Out of the Darkness – Into the Enchanted, and Beyond the Enchanted

About This Book

Hi! I am Cheryl Jacobs, owner of Kid's Party Characters.

Welcome to the Kid's Party Characters Guidebook for anyone who wants to make a living making kids happy. This book is for you if you are tired of the income you get on a day to day or week to week basis, and you have dreamed of owning your own company. I have been doing this for several years now and the process and business has changed, no, saved my life.

In my first book from the Darkness into the Enchanted I wrote about how and why I got into this business and now I show you how you can do the same.

The sections in this book are taken from my blog and show you how I developed the company and strategies over time, and now, I franchise out businesses with owners who want to do the same thing as I did.

You will never know the joy that children feel when your characters come to their party or visit them in the hospital. It's an impeccable feeling of contentment.

Contents

- About This Book 2
- My Story 6
- Three Things to Do in Your Business Daily 10
- Give Yourself Permission to Say No 17
  - While You are Creating Your Business 17
- The Kid's Party Characters Back Story 21
- Creating a Party Character Business 101 22
  - An Incredible Income OPportunity 22
- Business Tip: Tweak your thoughts and say NO. 24
  - A Strong BUsiness Mindset 24
- Business Tip: A Stress-Free Party starts Here 29
  - The First Step Toward Success 29
- How to Set and Achieve Goals in your New Business 32
  - THe Clear Path to Success 32
- Building a Successful Business 38
  - Finding Your Superpower 38
- Business Tip: The Boring is Necessary 43
  - So Get it Done First! 43
- Overcoming the Peter Pan Syndrome 50
  - Get Up and Get Started 50
- Parenting Tip: How to Raise an Entrepreneur 54
- Teaching Children about Safety 60
  - Expecially at Children's Parties 60
- Healthy Snacks and Party Food Ideas 67
  - Great Party Conversation 67
- Parent Tips: Balancing Work and Life 72
  - To Succeed in this Business 72

Parenting Tips: 10 Game IDEAS 75
    Some Great Party Ideas..75
Parenting Tip: Talking about Memorial Day............................84
    For Patriotic parties 84
In Closing...88

My Story

How I Began My Journey to Here

Taken from "Beyond the Enchanted"

As a child, around 7 or 8 years old was when I can remember total freedom and a sense of independence. I was the oldest of two sisters and a brother. I remember helping my mother a lot at this age. My brother and sisters were only one and two years of age at the time. It was when I first learned to change a diaper and babysit small children.

My formidable years formed the foundation of who I became as an adult. I felt an independence but at the same time, I felt that I had to grow up too fast. You know what I mean?

I remember my parents made a chore list and what the price for doing each chore got paid. Things like emptying all the garbage cans paid 50 cents. Vacuuming paid $1.00. For a 7-year-old in the 70s, making $5 a week was a lot of money.

I had a sister, Karen, only two years younger than me. We used to walk down to the end of the dead-end street and catch the bus to the elementary school. One year, I remember hearing "That damn school's roof was taken off by a tornado". I didn't know what that meant at the time, but it's a memory that has lived inside of me.

After school, my favorite thing to do was come home and watch the little rascals, then go play with my friends outside until dinner time. These are the most precious years of a child's life. Today I get to do parties for little ones this age and it makes me remember even more good times from my childhood days.

My father has this high-pitched whistle, ad when we heard it, we knew it was dinner time. All the kids in the neighborhood knew my dad's whistle.

Playing outside was the thing to do back then. There were no cell phones or internet. We rode bikes and big wheels everywhere. Climbed trees, build forts, played kick the can and swung on grapevines.

In the summer months when school was out, we were outside all day. There were so many apple trees, pecan trees, strawberry patches, blackberry bushes and grapevines we could eat fruit all day and not go home to eat.

I remember one day my dad loaded all of us kids and mom in the car and we went to this house that had a whole bunch of puppies. My dad picked this black, brown and white mixed puppy we named Pepper.

Every day I worked with Pepper. I taught him to sit, shake, lay down and roll over

I remember him pulling us by a rope on our big wheels and wagons all down the street.

He used to jump the fence and run away almost every day. One day, my dad told me he caught his little will on the top of the fence and he had to get the hose to set him free. One day he ran away never to return to us, and our mailman told us he got hit by a car.

We never got another dog after that.

Now around 9, my little brother and sister were four and five and sharing a room while me and Karen shared another. It was time to give everyone some space.

My dad then built an attached garage, living room and a bedroom for Karen and I above it. I always remember these spiral stairs going up to it. This room was overlooking the backyard.

I still to this day have dreams about the times I spent in that room. Karen and I slept there until I was 16 and her 14. It was the time from childhood to becoming a young lady.

At 16 my parents split, and I went to live with my dad. I didn't really get along too well with my mother growing up. I felt a resentment toward her.

I found myself always trying to prove myself to her. I was getting straight As and a trade and dreamed of being a country star. It seemed the better I did the more she resented me. As a young girl not getting approval from her mother, I was devastated. To this day, the abandonment issues have haunted me. I wanted so badly to have the acceptance of my mother.

By my senior year in high school I was the last girl in my class to have a boyfriend. Other kids would call me prude. So, to prove them wrong, I found a cute boy and asked him out, breaking up him and his current girlfriend. We dated for about six months, then he enlisted in the Air Force and I moved on. I felt I was too young to be with some boy forever. I dated a few other boys until I met my first husband. We actually were introduced at a funeral of a student who shot himself.

After only four months of dating my son was conceived in the driveway of my parents' house. I knew it when it happened. My boyfriend told me when he came inside of me, "He couldn't help himself." OMG! These words made me sick. It was like being raped.

Those words haunt me till this day. This is still rape.

I always felt he purposely strapped me to try to keep me from leaving him. I didn't tell my parents for a while. I didn't really have to. I was only an A-B cup breast size and all of a sudden, a full C. My mom knew right away. A mother's instincts are always right on.

I remember vividly the conversation with my mother and father. My mother doing all the talking, telling me since I'm Catholic, I couldn't have a child out of wedlock. My dad sat there with this look on his face, not saying a word.

Trapped now in the conundrum of having a baby, my life just went numb. I still blame my mother but slowly forgave it after my entire life. I encourage you to also forgive your parents, if you hold resentment for them for any reason.

We all make mistakes, as I will show you in the rest of this book. Our mistakes, while driven by our past experiences in the form of patterns, are ours to own. Take some time and create a path just for you, with total acceptance.

Throughout my life, every road led to another lesson, and every lesson led to another choice. Each choice helped pave the way for my career that became a 6-Figure business. I would not change a single thing about my path to get here, because I can now share my success story with you.

As you read the next few chapters in this Kindle book, keep a notebook with you to take down important "Ah Ha" moments. These little ideas that come into your mind, can be the very fuel you need to start your business and create the financial freedom you need while making children very happy.

We just opened a franchise in Houston, Texas. Are you next?

Three Things to Do in Your Business Daily

If you've thought about having your own business but haven't jumped in yet, you're likely stuck on the first question: Where do I start?

When you look at what other people with successful work from home businesses are doing, it can feel like you're looking at one of those 1000-piece puzzles where 90% of the pieces are green grass with tiny little variations in the shades of green that are enough to drive you insane.

Your new business can feel like that puzzle you don't have the time, patience, or even ability to put together.

If only you had a roadmap, imagine that.

What if each puzzle piece had a number on the back of it and all you had to do was connect the pieces by numerical order?

Your new business can be almost that easy, and we'll talk about how in just a minute.

But first let's dispel the myth that keeps most aspiring entrepreneurs from ever being successful or even giving it a try.

That myth is that your business is a 1000-piece puzzle.

It can be. If you want it to be. When you become more advanced. But the truth is, when you're starting out and trying to reach that first income goal, your business doesn't have to be any harder than those wooden shape puzzles with six different animals in them.

The ones where each animal has a small peg attached, and your toddler just has to figure out which hole each shape fits in.

The even better news is, your business puzzle only has three essential parts to it.

Yes, you can do more and you will do more.

But these are the three pieces that hold the puzzle together, so before you do anything else, make sure you're doing these three things.

1. Reach Out to Someone Personally Every Day

It's amazing how many entrepreneurs are introverts.

And finding this online gig is like the holy grail for introverts.

You don't actually have to *talk* to any real people. Instead you just post stuff online, and people grow to know, like, and trust you online, and they buy from you online.

Without you ever having to speak to them. Hallelujah.

While certainly there is that "make money while you sleep" aspect of your online business, the real magic comes from making money while you talk to people, especially as you're building your business.

This doesn't mean you have to call someone up and try to sell them your stuff every day.

It just means you have to reach out and connect with people.

Not even with the idea of selling them.

Just with the idea that the more people who know about you, the more people who will buy from you.

So what does it look like to reach out to someone personally?

It may mean messaging 10 of your LinkedIn connections and saying, "I do X, I see that you do Y, would you be interested in talking about how our businesses complement each other?"

Or, "I'm trying to build up a referral network of people I can trust. Would you like to talk more about what you do so I can add you to my network and send any potential clients your way?"

The point is just getting to know more people as people and not just website visitors, or social media followers.

You might reach out to someone who likes your content a lot, or someone whose content you like and just be real. Say, "I'm trying to get to know more people, wanna chat about our businesses for 20 minutes on Zoom?"

The only agenda here is to make a personal connection with people.

Those people may never become customers, but some will, and more importantly it will open unknown doors for you and put you top of mind when it comes to others referring you.

2. **Put a Buy Button in Front of Someone Every Day**

This is a huge mistake that even many seasoned business owners make.

So, you've got this great product or service, and you've even set up a little website, and you're posting on social media to build your audience.

But how many people are actually seeing something from you each day that includes a "buy now" button they can click on and actually send you money?

I hear you protesting, "But I can't sell on social media, everyone will hate me and unfollow me."

To a point, you are right. Not every social media post should be a blatant sales pitch. We all hate that.

But if you're adding value to your social media connections, you should also be consistently, gently, offering them a link where they can go check out what you're selling.

And, remember your business doesn't just live on social media.

Build an email list and you can put a link to your buy button in every single email you send. Again, just make sure you're adding some value, so they'll actually open your emails.

How you'll get your buy button in front of people is going to be different for different people. You may use some paid ads or start a Facebook group and have links to your products and services pinned to the top, or drive people to your offers through blogging, or posting YouTube videos.

There are a number of ways to do it, and you should be using more than one of them.

The point is, don't think your job is done for the day because you've created some content and posted it on three social media networks.

Your day is not done until you've gotten some eyes on a buy button.

3. Take at Least One Step Towards Your Goals Every Day

You have to actively monitor yourself each day in your business or you can find that weeks, and then months, go by and you're still stuck in the same place you were when you started your business.

Once you have your business and life goals mapped out (which is another discussion for a different day), when you're planning your day you need to ask yourself: "What step(s) am I taking today to bring myself closer to my goal of making $1000 this month?" Or launching a new product this month, or signing on 3 new clients this month, whatever the goal is.

And at the end of the day, you need to again ask yourself, what steps did I take today to get closer to that goal?

It's easy to get lost in doing the fun things in your business, and in doing the boring admin stuff in your business, and in running around on the internet all day in the name of working, only to discover at the end of the day you've made no progress toward your ultimate goals for your business and your life.

Checking in with yourself and having the right to-do list are essential to making sure you're not just spinning your wheels.

But How Do I Make All This Happen?

Okay, it's only three things, but if you're a new or struggling business owner, you may be saying, "But I don't know how to reach out to people, or how to even get a buy button up, or what good, realistic goals look like."

Remember how we talked earlier about making your business as easy as a puzzle with numbers on the back?

While that may be a bit of an over-simplification, you can take 90% of the stress and stumbling out of your business by having a business mentor.

Your mentor can't do it all for you, and you have to make some mistakes along the way if you want to grow into your greatness.

But a mentor can be, and often is, the key difference in those who find success in their business and those who throw in the towel.

So, you can go out and do these three things on your own, learning by trial and error, or you can save time, money, and your sanity by hooking up with a mentor.

I began with nothing but two beautiful babies who needed to be fed and has since started 10 businesses, including Kids Party Characters, which she runs from home and has turned into a six-figure venture.

With a license, you have the right to book parties in an exclusive territory, access to over 200 of our unique costumes as well as our casting director and acting coach.

Every Day this Could Be You!

Give Yourself Permission to Say No

WHILE YOU ARE CREATING YOUR BUSINESS

Yesterday we talked about the power of learning to say "no" to people when you're a small business owner. You can catch up right here if you missed it. Truth is, as stay at home moms, our first hurdle is often learning how to say "yes" to ourselves.

Part of the mom gene includes putting others first. And with kids, putting even one child first is a full-time job.

The result is that we often end up with little or no time for what we really want to be in life.

We try to make ourselves feel better in the self-care department by saying, well, I go to the gym three times a week, I had a massage last month, I took a knitting class at the community college.

These things are all great, but...For many of us moms, we feel like we have a more significant mark to leave on the world than "greatest soccer mom," or "provider of the best afternoon snack for the whole neighborhood."

And so, we tell ourselves that when our kids get older we'll try to re-enter the work force, or maybe start that business that runs through our head as we're contemplating what talents we have beyond diaper changing and family mediator.

If this describes you, then you're about to get some good news, although it may make you feel uncomfortable, and you may even think "I can't do that" at first.

You don't have to, and you shouldn't, wait another day to say "yes" to yourself.

Throw Away the Buts

The time to start your own business is today.

As you read that, if you find yourself saying, "But," followed by *any* excuse, then it's time for you to shed your buts.

Every single "but" you have is like a 10-pound weight you're carrying around on your back.

Your "buts" are literally weighing you down and stopping you from taking the action that you need to so that you can step into your greatness today.

The good news is, you have the power to throw every one of those "buts" off your back. Not a one of them is permanently affixed there, no matter what you currently think.

Taking the First Step into Greatness

Martin Luther King, Jr. said, "Faith is taking the first step even when you don't see the whole staircase."

This describes what your first step will be like.

You may feel like you're different, like your "buts" *are* permanently cemented on your back.

That's common. It just means that in the beginning, you'll have to have faith that you can shed the excuses and get that business going today.

The first step to making any significant change is to silence the inner and outer critics and to firmly decide that you're going to make it happen.

Why Not Wait?

But wouldn't it be easier to just wait?

Wait until the buts fall off by themselves.

Until the kids are in school or grown, until your partner gets a raise and you're more financially secure, until you've moved into a house that better fits your needs.

There are at least two problems with waiting.

First, if you wait for the excuses to resolve themselves, you'll die before you get started.

Reality is, there's always an excuse.

Second, do you really *want* to wait?

Does the thought of having your own business where you're doing something you love that benefits others and they're paying you for it excite you?

If yes, then why would you want to wait to fulfill this urge, goal, dream, whatever it is for you?

When Mama's Happy, Everyone's Happy

You've probably heard the quote "If Mama ain't happy, ain't nobody happy."

It's a popular quote because there's a lot of truth to it!

So, if one of your "buts" is that you don't want to take time away from meeting your kids' needs, give this quote some thought.

You are your child's greatest role model, like it or not. As a parent, or as an owner of a Franchise you are a role model.

When she sees how much excitement and satisfaction you get out of working your business, she will share your happiness.

Think of your business as a gift you're giving to your whole family.

In addition to the personal satisfaction you'll get from it, there's also the extra income to get excited about.

And feeling good about the money piece doesn't make you a sleazy salesperson.

You're giving value in exchange for money and that's what makes the world spin.

This may buy your kids a few extra non-essential items, free up some financial tension in the household, or open up a whole new world of experiences you'd love to treat your kids to but couldn't swing in the past.

This All Sounds Really Great, But

You may still have some "buts" swirling around in your head.

Kind of like when you go to the motivationally-charged Amway meeting but realize in the car on the way home that you really have no idea how to sell this stuff, and no one to sell it to anyway.

If you're ready to step into your greatness today, if you're willing to take that first step in faith and *decide* that you can do it, then we're ready to help you here at KidsPartyCharacters.com.

Don't know how you'll find a couple extra hours in your day to run a business? We've got you covered.

Not sure what the first step to getting started is? We'll lead you by the hand.

Wondering how you'd get anyone to notice your business? We're experts at that too.

The Kid's Party Characters Back Story

In my book, "Out of the Darkness – Into the Enchanted" I revealed some very vulnerable parts of myself including how I started Kid's Party Characters. Being a single mom was not easy and it led me down many roads, with as many bad choices in men and career.

When I started this business, I had actually been working as an actress with another company that did the same thing. I fell in love with watching the children shine so much joy into the world that I decided I wanted to do it myself. That was the greatest choice I have ever made.

I continued learning all I could about business, attended numerous Tony Robbins events and got coached by the greatest. I gained friends and lost them as they could not stay with me through the growth. I hope you will see that you can use the skills in this book to not only make a living helping kids find joy, but really make the money you need to achieve financial freedom in your life.

Creating a Party Character Business 101

AN INCREDIBLE INCOME OPPORTUNITY

http://www.KidsPartyCharacters.com

What the business does.

One of the things that we do at Kid's Party Characters is go to parties for kids and we also go out to hospitals and assist with the Make a Wish foundation to help kids with chronic and life-threatening diseases feel just a little better about their lives.

The administration of this business.

Each day we take calls, collect money and send out actors out on jobs with their costumes and instructions. When they are there, their job is to entertain and cause laughter. They play the role so well, that sometimes I don't even know they are not real. This is the greatest part of this business.

Finding and Hiring Actors

I must have interviewed 100's of people when I first started the company, but my former jobs as a talent scout prepared me for this activity. I can tell from the voices and attitudes which actors will be good for kid's characters and which ones would not. For example, you don't want someone who feels any animosity toward children, under a costume that could scare a child. Just use your intuition.

Obtaining the Costumes

With your franchise membership you receive access to over 200 costumes but you can choose to procure your own. There may be a character we have not thought of that you think would help your business. There are several ways to obtain the costumes for your Kid's Party Character business. Many times, you can find companies that are going out of business, and you can also find the costumes at many online stores that deliver quickly.

Business Tip: Tweak your thoughts and say NO.

A STRONG BUSINESS MINDSET

When your business is new, or not yet making a consistent income, it's common to have thoughts like, "I'd do anything for more customers." In this business you will be bombarded with people who want to get your service free. This must be avoided at all costs.

While this willingness to work hard and openness to exploring less than desirable ways to grow your business is admirable, it can also be deadly and counterproductive to your business.

It's true that you won't be able to be as picky about who you take money from and provide service to in the beginning as you will once you have more customers than you can handle.

But, it's super important for the longevity of your business, and for your sanity, that you learn this simple word early on: No.

Technically, it's easy to say "no." As a parent, it's almost an automatic response that comes out of your mouth as soon your child opens her mouth some days!

But as a new business owner, you can find it almost impossible to say "no" when faced with any opportunity that might make you more money.

Today we're going to uncover the formula for always knowing when "no" is the right answer, and look at some of the common situations where business owners often say "yes" when they should be saying "no."

How to Always Know Your No

In the simplest way, it comes down to this: When you're clear on your "yes," it becomes easy to say "no."

What exactly does that mean?

It means that when you know what you want, and have crystallized what your goals, values, and morals are personally and for your business, knowing when to say "no" becomes much easier,

Which means "no" will come out of your mouth quicker and with much greater confidence.

The best way to always know your "no," is to develop a mission statement for your business.

Initially this may feel a little weird, you're just one person, trying to build your dream business, not some big company with thousands of employees trying to change the world and needing to get everyone on the same page to do it.

But unlike many big companies, who have mission statements for the benefit of their customers, your mission statement is really more for *you* right now.

It's to keep you on track and headed in the right direction so that your business does grow into what your dream is, and doesn't get derailed into either a job you hate, or a hobby that costs instead of makes you money.

Your mission statement should include a summary of the value your business provides, and the core values you abide by to deliver that value while still operating as a business and not a charity.

If you need help getting started, check out [these 27 examples](#) of big brand mission statements.

Just remember in looking at some of these examples, that while the goal of the big brand may be to come up with a flashy one-liner that sounds good to customers, your goal for now anyway is clarity, which is going to require more than a sentence.

When your mission statement is complete, you should be able to read it in any situation you're faced with and know exactly whether your response is a "yes" or a "no."

Common Mistakes Small Business Owners Make

There are a few things most everyone gets wrong when they're starting out.

These are tempting "yeses" that should always be a definitive "no."

Can I Get a Discount?

This is an especially big problem if marketing your product or service requires you to get on the phone with the potential client before the sale is complete.

But even if you have a product or service with a "buy now" button right there on your sales page, you'll still get people emailing you about getting a discount or coupon code.

And then there's the ever popular, "Can I pay you after I make some money," or see whatever positive result comes from your product.

Don't be shamed into the common logic these freeloaders use of, "Well, if it works the way you say it does, you have nothing to worry about, you'll get your money."

Customers who want something for nothing or who are always gaming for a discount are *never* worth the ensuing hassle they'll create.

Just say no.

Now if *you* want to offer some kind of a discount or freebie as a promotion or in an effort to get exposure or testimonials for your service, that's another thing.

Just make sure the discount is always your idea and on your terms.

For $1997 I Can Show You How to Get More Free Traffic Than You Can Handle

Unfortunately, new business owners are a dream for many an unscrupulous marketer out there.

This is the "how to make money online" crowd, whose mission statement is to sell everyone as much information as they can regardless of whether it's good information and regardless of whether you need it in your business right now.

Once you become a small business owner, you somehow become a magnet for these types.

The old adage of "if it sounds too good to be true, it probably is" applies here.

Ignore their sales pages, unfollow them on social media, and unsubscribe from their email lists.

When it comes to anyone who wants to sell you a magic button solution for growing your business bigger and faster, just say no.

I Will Make Sure No One Ever Buys From You Again

Refuse to engage with anyone who bullies or trolls you online. Ban them, block them, erase them from your life.

This may seem like an obvious point, but it can be difficult when you're starting out because you tend to be a little desperate for customers and you are definitely concerned about establishing and maintaining a positive reputation.

If someone is publicly harassing you online, politely invite them to direct message or email you and see if you can resolve whatever the situation is.

If they continue, have no tolerance for their behavior and whatever you do, *do not* engage in public bickering with them.

Don't worry about their crazy threats to expose you for the fraud you are or make sure no one ever buys from you again, the rest of the sane world sees what you're going through and sympathizes with you, not the troll.

In some instances, it will help here to have a clear and very public refund policy.

And don't hesitate to use it. Disgruntled customers cost you way more money than they've ever paid you.

Also, don't hesitate to go outside of your refund policy and refund someone even if they don't ask when it's clear that they're more trouble than they're worth.

Simply issue the refund and send them a kind note about how it's not going to work out, but you wish them the best of luck.

Finally, be careful about who you take money from to begin with.

No matter how bad you think you need customers, if you have that bad feeling in your stomach about this one, send him on his way before he even has a chance to become a client.

Kids Party Characters is Here to Help

No one builds a successful business alone.

As with most things in your business, it's best to have a mentor who can help you make the right decisions - and avoid all the wrong ones - so you don't have to waste hundreds of hours and thousands of dollars on trying to figure out how to make your business work.

Yes, you can always read your mission statement and determine whether something's a "yes" or a "no" for you based on that, even experienced business owners operate this way.

But what if you had someone with business experience and expertise who could guide you through the hard stuff and get you into profit sooner rather than later?

Business Tip: A Stress-Free Party starts Here

THE FIRST STEP TOWARD SUCCESS

For many children, there are few things more anticipated than their birthday party. Children think about their birthday year-round, and have ever-changing ideas about having the perfect party that would rival Cinderella's ball in it's grandiosity.

To make all the excitement translate into a party as perfect in reality as it was in your child's imagination, can be quite a task. However, with a little conscious planning, you can pull off a birthday party that will be fun and memorable for you, your child, and her guests.

Here are five tips to make sure your child's party is as stress-free for everyone as it is fun.

1. **Don't Go Overboard**: Be realistic about what you can do and what your child and her guests can handle. While your child may have a hundred ideas running around in her head, remember that she is going to have fun simply getting together with her friends in celebration of her birthday.

If you try to do too much, or create too much hype about this being the party of the century, it's bound to lead to some overwhelm and/or let down when it comes to the actual event.

Talk with your child about what things are really important to her and make wise decisions about going with her top two or three ideas that feel realistic and fun for her personality and age. Remember that in day-to-day life as parents we make choices about which of our children's wishes are granted, and apply this to party planning too.

2. **Be Conscious of the Time of Day and Length of the Party**: As adults, we can party all night! The same does *not* hold true for children. After a certain amount of time, the fun is going to turn into

exhaustion and crankiness. The last thing you want is for what started out as laughter and fun memory-making, to end in bickering and tears.

Always have a set ending time for the party. For most ages, don't make the party last longer than two hours. In planning, this may seem short to cram everything in, but remember tip number one, and resist the urge to plan too much.

Consider having the party earlier in the day rather than late afternoon when even older children start to get a little tired. For younger kids, definitely plan around nap time.

3. **Have a Plan**: Plan the party to fit within the space you have. If you're holding the party at a shelter in the park, you may not have to have much of a plan at all, as the playground will provide as much entertainment as you need. You can also have some jump ropes and balls available, or organize a game of tag to take advantage of your outdoor spaces.

If you have a more confined indoor space, don't plan overly lively activities that will cause a lot of noise and commotion. This is when some of the children may feel stressed or anxious and tempers will start to flare.

Offer the children a couple of choices at your indoor party, and make sure everyone is invited to be included, but not forced to participate. Gauge the personalities of your child and his friends. You may want to offer a game of musical chairs, and also have a craft going on for the less competitive child.

Don't plan too many activities, as you want the children to feel relaxed and not rushed to get through everything before being pushed out the door. And if you don't get to something, don't worry about it. Go with the flow of the party and be aware of the mood in the room so you can adjust accordingly.

4. **Open Gifts After the Party**: For starters, there really isn't time to open gifts during the party. In addition, the excitement of the new toys can cause jealousy among the children who all want to see and open and play with each gift, or have their gift opened first by your child.

Saving gift opening for the privacy of after the party can avoid hurt feelings if one child's gift isn't as well received. It will also avoid any negative comments your birthday boy might publicly make, since children of all ages are lacking in the filter of what's socially appropriate at times.

Make sure your child sends a nice, personalized thank you note so his guests will know the gift was appreciated and enjoyed. You may include a picture of your child with the gift or let even the youngest of children at least help in writing or designing the thank you note.

5. **Communication is Key**: Communicate early and often with all of the service providers involved in making the party happen, including the party venue and any rentals and catering that are involved. Be clear about what your expectations are and know what the providers' expectations are.

Ask questions if you have them, don't assume the way you think things should be. Double check that everything's in place and on target a day or two before the party.

Work with experienced companies like kidspartycharacters.com, who have a history of demonstrating their love for making your child's party exceed her expectations.

At kidspartycharacters.com, we can eliminate the stress of dealing with several different companies by taking care of all your entertainment needs. We have packages that include over 200 of your child's favorite characters, as well as balloon artists and face painting. Our goal is to make your child's party magical for him and easy for you.

Find out how hassle-free your party can be with just a phone call or a few clicks of the mouse by visiting kidspartycharacters.com, and get started making your child's next party dreams come true today.

Need some ideas and inspiration? Connect with us on Facebook to take a look at some of the fun parties we've helped bring to life.

How to Set and Achieve Goals in your New Business

THE CLEAR PATH TO SUCCESS

Chances are, you're not new to goal setting, even if the only experience you have with it is setting the ever-popular yet rarely successful New Year's resolutions.

Even if your experience with goal setting hasn't always delivered the life-changing results you'd hoped for, don't let that discourage you from the possibilities goal setting offers.

All the evidence shows that, *when done right*, goal setting is a required activity if you want to have what you want to have in your life.

Aside from your personal goals, having goals specific to the growth and performance of your business will motivate you to action, keep you accountable, and warn you when you've gotten off track.

So, whether you're just thinking about starting a business, already have a business that's struggling, or just want your business to soar to even higher levels, here's a blueprint for structuring goals that will help you build a business that makes you happy and makes you money.

When you set your goals, you'll want to set them based on what you commit to doing over the next 90 days.

90 days gives you enough time to accomplish a lot, but not so much time that you procrastinate because the deadline seems so far away.

Basically, there are four areas in which you should be setting goals: Money, Marketing, Products, and People.

Your goals will grow and expand from here, but let's look at good starting points.

Money Goals

This one's pretty straight-forward — How much money do you want to make?

But it's not quite that easy to figure out.

Obviously, how much money you want to make today will be different than how much money you'll want to make in a year or five years, and beyond.

The trick here is to be realistic, yet not too limiting.

And, often when you're starting out, your answer is, "I don't know, as much as I can," because you really don't know what a good number is.

If you have an amount you **need** to make, that's a good place to start.

If you need to pay the mortgage and certain bills from your business right out the gate, that number will become your initial money goal.

If you have a little more flexibility, start with how much your product or service costs and how many you'd like to sell per month.

The number should be a little scary, but not something you can't in a million years realistically imagine achieving over the next 90 days.

Marketing Goals

How are you going to sell your product or service?

The good news and the bad news is that there are a hundred different ways to market your business.

In the beginning, you'll want to do them all and feel like you have to do them all to grow a successful business.

But in reality, that's the quickest path to failure.

Don't spread yourself or your money too thin.

Pick one or two ways you want to market your business in the beginning.

Maybe money is tight and you'll choose to do a lot of in-person networking and referrals for your first marketing goals.

After you've mastered that and some money is coming in, having a website designed and doing some paid advertising may be the focus of your next goal setting period.

Start with what you can and want to do, and make all your goals around that marketing strategy.

If you're doing networking for the next 90 days, set goals for how many groups you'll join, how many people you'll talk to each day, how many events you'll attend each week, what kinds of things you'll share with people about your business and how those conversations will go.

Product Goals

What products and services do you want to offer in your business?

Starting out, most people have one, and maybe that's all you can imagine for now.

If you're just going to focus on your one product or service over the next 90 days, that's fine, just make your goals around how you're going to improve upon that product or how you'll package it for marketing, or how you'll talk to people about it.

As you become a more experienced and savvy business owner, you'll get new product ideas or find affiliate products you'll want to sell.

If you offer a service, you'll come up with ways to package that service and offer it to groups or as some type of a home study course.

Even if your goals focus on one product or service right now, maybe in the next 90 days you want to develop an outline for a second offering, or make a list a people in your market you'd like to do a joint venture with.

In other words, even if you aren't rolling out something new over the next 90 days, you could have the beginnings of it in the works.

People Goals

Here's something you may not fully understand yet.

Even though you are the sole owner of your own business and have no employees, you cannot, will not, and should not try to do this entrepreneurship thing on your own.

It doesn't work.

Your people goals should be two-fold: Who do you want to connect with, and who do you want to hire.

First, who do you want to connect with?

This may be others in your market you admire, or have noticed are farther along than you and you'd like to see how you can help them in exchange for hanging out with them and soaking up some of their knowledge.

If may be a group of peers you want to meet up with virtually or in real life for support and brainstorming, or it may be a paid mastermind you want to join, or it could be as simple as reaching out to some of your LinkedIn connections.

Whatever the case, there should always be people on your radar who you're looking to connect with for the mutual benefit of both of you.

Second, who do you want to hire?

And this doesn't mean you have to bring on employees. You can go your whole business life just outsourcing to independent contractors and not having any employees.

Whatever the case, you want to be constantly looking at your business and figuring out what you could pay someone else to do so that you don't have to do it.

Start with your weaknesses, what's hard for you and what do you not enjoy doing?

If you don't like the tech side of your business (most of us don't!) outsource all of your website, and landing page, and autoresponder, and setting anything up online duties to someone who gets great joy out of such activities.

Yes, those people do exist, and they can make your life SO much easier!

If you're thinking it will be forever before you have enough money to do this, know that you can start small.

You can spend $100 having a VA do some busy work for you, or even $20 having someone on Fiverr create some graphics for you.

And if all of this is sounding foreign to you right now, don't worry. Within your first 90 days it will all make sense and you'll be excited at the possibility of paying someone to do these things for you.

Need Help?

As you likely know, one of the best ways to ensure your business success is to work with a mentor.

The experience your mentor brings to the table helps you set better goals, reach them faster, and readjust course when things aren't going right.

Kids Party Characters owner Cheryl Jacobs has started 10 businesses, and successfully operates three of them today.

Because she started as a single mom with two young children and no resources, and had to work her way to success through trial and error, Cheryl has a soft spot for other moms who stay home with their children but would like to either create some extra income, or need to create some income to provide for their families.

Cheryl's created a unique opportunity to have your very own membership to KidsPartyCharacters.com.

Membership basically hands you a business that you can start generating income with very quickly, without all the setup and struggles most business owners face.

With your KidsPartyCharacters.com membership, you'll receive an exclusive territory in which to book parties, the right to use our 200 plus costumes, access to our casting director and acting coach, and business training and support from Cheryl and the team at Kids Party Characters.

If this seems like an opportunity that could be the answer to your entrepreneurial callings, or if you simply have more questions, book a call with Cheryl today and she'll help you figure it all out. The call is free, there's no pressure or sales pitch, it's simply Cheryl's way of extending a helping hand to fellow moms and entrepreneurs.

Learn more about the magic we bring to life at children's parties throughout the year by joining us on Facebook for daily updates.

Building a Successful Business

FINDING YOUR SUPERPOWER

If you know much about Kids Party Characters, you're probably familiar with the story of owner Cheryl Jacobs and how she came to be a successful entrepreneur.

Most people who looked at Cheryl's life when she was younger would have predicted a life of struggle and poverty for her.

Married to her high school sweetheart at the age of 18, she was blessed with two wonderful kids by the time she was 19, but an abusive husband that clouded the picture of a happy family.

She soon found herself a young single mother forced to rely on the generosity of local churches just to meet the basic food needs of her family.

Many would have adopted this victim role as a way of life and ended up on state assistance with minimum wage jobs, at best, for the rest of their lives.

But Cheryl wanted more than that for herself and her children.

As a result of her hard work, Cheryl was able to land a modeling contract that set her life down a path of serial entrepreneurship and financial freedom.

Fast forward to today and Cheryl has owned 10 businesses, currently runs three businesses, and lives life on her terms in sharp contrast to the days when she had to eat whatever others could find for her.

If you're an entrepreneur or are at all familiar with the story of any successful business owner, you probably know that

Cheryl's "rags to riches" saga is not unfamiliar in the world of entrepreneurship.

Many successful business owners, in fact it seems most successful business owners, have overcome great obstacles and setbacks to get where they are today.

While we all love to hear these stories and commend the women and men behind them, it can leave you thinking, "Do I have what it takes to be a successful business owner?"

Let's face it, it took some superpowers for Cheryl to do a complete 180 in her life.

And if you've never lived in such dire circumstances, you might wonder if the familiar refrain of, "If I can do it, so can you," is really true when it comes to entrepreneurship.

Fortunately, you don't have to have seen desperate times to build a successful business.

Unfortunately, being a business owner isn't the right move for everyone, as appealing as the time and financial freedom is to all of us.

How do you know if it's the right move for you?

Well, the best way is to schedule a call with Cheryl, who has a gift for mentoring other entrepreneurs, and let her walk you through how she can help you get started and be successful. Before you do that though, let's make sure you do in fact have the characteristics many don't that are crucial for entrepreneurship.

While there are many traits that will serve you well as an entrepreneur, here are three of the biggest "must haves" if you're considering starting your own business.

Passion

A lot of people who start a business go into it with more of a "hobby" attitude than a "business" attitude.

They're going to play around with it and see if it works, basically.

It won't.

You may have heard that you should start a business around something you're passionate about if you want to be successful, and that if you do, you'll never have to work another day in your life.

That's partly true, but does over-romanticize business ownership a bit.

It's great if you have a thing you're passionate about and want your business to be all about selling that particular product or service, but it's not required.

What is required is that you're passionate about making your business successful, whatever your "why" is.

It could be that you really do love your product or service.

It could be that you're like Cheryl was, and are desperately looking for some way to provide for your family.

Or maybe you're doing okay, but just can't imagine going your whole life without traveling around the world, something your current job will never allow for.

Whatever your "why" is, there has to be one that makes you passionate about finding a worthy product or service that you'd be happy to attach your name to.

Persistence

Now, about that "you'll never work another day in your life" thing.

If only it were true!

You know, no matter how much you love what you do, building and running your own business is going to require some work.

A lot of work in the initial stages. And those "initial stages" could last a year or two.

If you're the kind of person who feels like you'd like to try a business to see if it works, you either need to rethink things, or stick with your job.

No business bursts out of the gates wildly successful and never looks back.

It usually takes some time to get that first sale.

Or maybe you'll have a $10,000 launch and zero sales in month two.

There are hiccups, failures, changes in circumstances, and unforeseen roadblocks in every business.

You simply have to be persistent in the face of these things, driven by your passion, or you might as well not waste your time and money getting started.

Without persistence, you either end up with an expensive hobby, floating from business to business with no real success, or quitting all together, broke and discouraged, at what you deemed a failure, but what likely didn't have to be an ending point.

Sense of Adventure

Business ownership is not for the weak of heart, as you can probably already tell.

You're going to have to get out of your comfort zone and do some things you haven't done, learn some things that seem too hard, take some risks that may not pay off.

This doesn't mean you'll have to live outside your comfort zone, who wants to do that?

But it does mean you'll likely have to expand your comfort zone and welcome some new things into it.

Many new business owners are creatives and are very uncomfortable with the techie side of having an online business.

While you can outsource most of that to other people, you're going to need to have some basic understanding, at least, of some things you otherwise would have no interest in learning.

Of course this is not to say you should even consider doing anything illegal or immoral in your eyes, but you will need to develop a reaction of, "Sure, I can try/learn/do that," with things that make you uncomfortable in the sense that you think they're above you, they bore you, or they scare you.

Being an entrepreneur requires putting yourself out there, and that's scary to most of us.

With membership, you get an exclusive territory in which to book parties, the right to use our 200+ costumes, and access to our casting director and acting coach.

In addition, you get business training and support from Cheryl and all the team at Kids Party Characters.

Business Tip: The Boring is Necessary

SO GET IT DONE FIRST!

As you begin to formulate just how you can make this opportunity work for you, then you must have an idea of all of the parts, even the really boring ones like planning your marketing and branding.

If you're undecided on whether you really need this information, don't click away yet, as the answer might surprise you. A lot of small business owners don't give branding a second thought, dismissing it as something only the big companies have to worry about.

There are two reasons this attitude is wrong and will be costly if not deadly for your small business. First, big companies have lots of money to throw at getting people to notice them, you don't (yet anyway!).

So, if you want to stand out and get the attention of your potential customers, those people who need what you've got, you're going to need to have a strong brand.

Second, whether you like it or not, your small business will have a brand,

To understand this, it may help to think of your business brand as your reputation, or the impression you leave on people, or the experience you provide customers, because that's really what it comes down to.

If we ask the question differently then, "Do you want to create a strong reputation for your small business?" the answer is going to be a resounding yes.

While you may not need to become the Kleenex of the tissue industry, or the Pampers of the diaper industry, you do need to have a reputation, or brand, that draws people to you over their other options.

Let's take a look at the steps to developing such a brand.

1. Know Your Avatars

Avatar is another word for ideal customer.

You can't, and don't need to market to the whole world.

For example, here at [Kids Party Characters](), when it comes to people who don't have kids, we don't care much whether our marketing and our brand resonates with them.

If you've been around at all, you may have seen advice that promotes having one avatar, that ideal, dream-come-true customer that you wish would walk through your virtual door a hundred times a day.

Reality is, almost every business has more than one ideal client.

For example, it may be that you serve women just as well as men, or 30 year olds just as well as 50 year olds.

Don't limit yourself to one avatar, but do come up with two or three people, if you need, who would be your ideal customers.

Describe them in as much detail as you can and give them each a name. These are the individuals you'll be talking to when you're creating the rest of your branding and delivering your message.

And if you'll think of it in terms of talking to another person rather than just "putting it out there," it's much easier to craft a compelling message.

2. Establish What You Stand For

What you stand for is a combination of your mission statement, your values, and your goals.

This will be an internal document, not something you publish or give to customers.

It's more like a brainstorming activity to determine what's important to you and what your messaging around it will be.

Basically, when someone says, "X Company, they're the ones that _____," how do you want her to be filling in that blank?

3. Focus on Standing Out

Once you've determined what you stand for, how will you use that to make your business stand out?

You may have seen this referred to as your USP, or unique selling proposition.

You're going to need to be memorable, have some fact, or mission, or trait about your business that makes you different from your potential customers' other choices.

This can be difficult to determine. New business owners especially, often think they do what others in their market do, they just aim to do it better.

Of course that's not enough, everyone claims to be the best.

What makes you unique and causes you to stand out doesn't have to be directly related to your product or service.

For example, maybe what makes your business most memorable to people is that it was started by a single mom raising two kids, working nights at her kitchen table after coming home from a stressful, under-paying day job.

Make sure you focus on one thing here.

If you try to stand out because you have the highest quality, most reliable service, cheapest prices, and most innovative products, you'll dilute your message into oblivion.

It's much easier for people to remember you for one thing.

4. Decide How You'll Deliver Your Message

All of your marketing and communications with prospects and customers should be delivered in the same tone of voice.

Your voice is heard in both the language you use and the personality with which you deliver your messages.

Are you going to be formal and conservative? Funny and a little controversial at times? Would you ever write "C U later" instead of "see you later?"

Every communication you have should resonate with your audience as, "that sounds like something she'd say."

If you have employees, VAs, ghostwriters, or other outsourcers, make sure they are speaking the same language you do when communicating on behalf of your business.

5. Create a Feeling

This one's about having a logo, color scheme, and fonts that are present across everything you do, whether it's your website, advertising, emails, social media, or written correspondence.

The goal is that when people see something that's yours, they recognize it as coming from you before they ever see your name on it.

Don't fret if money is tight right now.

Yes, ideally, you'd hire a designer and she'd come up with a color scheme, logo, website, and custom graphics for all of your social media platforms.

But you can easily DIY most of this, and get a passable logo and even social media graphics done very cheaply at Fiverr.

To come up with your color scheme, spend a little time at Color.co. (Be careful, it can be addictive!) They have thousands of pre-designed color schemes, or you can create your own from scratch.

You'll need at least the color scheme in place when you go to design anything yourself, or hand things off to an independent designer.

And if you're thinking you could never in a million years create your own graphics, spend a couple of hours on Canva and you might surprise yourself.

It likely won't be to "professional," but simple rules the day anymore, and you'll be surprised what you can create with the tools Canva provides, no matter how challenged and inexperienced you are.

6. Be Consistent

You can't develop a strong brand if no one's ever hearing from you.

Decide how you're going to communicate with your audience and do it every day.

Do some research to figure out where your people hang out the most, but generally, you can't go wrong by choosing some combination of social media, email marketing, newsletters, podcasting, physical mailings, and videos.

This one's simple and straightforward, but is probably the most common place where small business drop the ball.

7. Deliver Value

Finally, you can get all the above right and still fail miserably if your business doesn't deliver a consistently valuable product or service along with a valuable message to your market.

So, the first part is obvious, make sure what you're selling is worth more than what your customers are paying for it.

If you're failing in this area, your customers and your refund rate will let you know.

As for the valuable message, when communicating with your market, be conscious of how much selling you're doing as opposed to how much value you're delivering.

In other words, give to your customers more than you take.

If your audience is seeing an email or social media post from you every day that does nothing but sell your product or service, they're going to tune out.

On the other hand, if your communications contain some knowledge, information, tip, or strategy that helps them, people will make a habit of reading what you say, and some days they'll click on the link at the end that takes them to your product or service.

Want a Head Start in Your Business?

If it feels like this whole branding thing takes a lot of time and effort, you're right, it does.

it's actually one of those things that's an ongoing part of your daily business activities.

So how can your shortcut your branding efforts so you can focus on the important stuff like serving customers and making money?

The easiest way is to start with a business that already has a great brand.

And that's exactly what you get when you buy a membership to KidsPartyCharacters.com.

Membership gives you your very own Kids Party Character business, which means you're starting on day one with a business that has a strong, established brand in the children's entertainment industry for providing engaging, professional entertainment at kids' parties by the child's most-loved characters.

Your membership gives you license to use our 200 plus costumes, access to our acting coach and casting director, an exclusive territory in which to book parties, and business training and support from Cheryl Jacobs and the Kids Party Characters team.

Overcoming the Peter Pan Syndrome

GET UP AND GET STARTED

Ever wake up in the morning with thoughts of "I don't wanna grow up!?" Let's face it, adulting can be hard. Peter Pan had a point when he declared, "I won't grow up! 'Cause growing up is awfuller than all the awful things that ever were."

We all have those certain days when we'd give anything to snuggle in with a fuzzy stuffed animal and sleep the day away, or to spend the day in a make believe world of dolls, trains, and building blocks.

So while it can be very frustrating when our children resist some of the added responsibilities that come with growing up, it will be easier on them, and on you as the parent, if you try to relate to their feelings rather than coming at them with a "too bad, life is hard" sort of attitude.

There are three things you can do that will help your child conquer Peter Pan syndrome and make life easier for everyone in your family.

First, Start When Your Children are Young

Ever find yourself saying to your children something like, "You're old enough to clean the toilet now?" Put that way, who among us wouldn't react with "I won't grow up!?"

If you start giving your child age appropriate responsibilities early on, you can avoid bringing on a mindset that growing up involves doing all kinds of undesirable things. This will go a long ways towards eliminating a lot of the pushback you'll get from your kids when you add responsibilities and expectations.

For example, a child who is two can be taught how to use a clothes hamper, and that special place we put our shoes when we take them off.

A child who is three can take on small tasks like feeding the dog. These may require a little help from mom or dad, but that's all the better since your child still thinks you're cool at this age and likes to follow you around and be helpful.

Second, Tie Bigger Responsibilities to a Positive Consequence

You may not be a fan of providing rewards for things that your children should be expected to do as humans contributing to your family and the larger society. That's good, because that's not what you'll be doing here.

It's a fact of life that many undesirable things we do have a positive consequence, and that's why we do them. We don't like to clean the toilet, but "Eewww" if we never do.

Now with kids, it's a little different. Most kids have no problem with a dirty toilet, a messy room, a hungry dog . . .

So, you'll have to be a little creative with what the positive consequence of the behavior is. To do this, it's best to think like your child. If he loves to ride his scooter all over the house, approach clean up by saying, "This would be a great time to ride your scooter, let's get everything off the floor so you have plenty of room to do that."

With older children, consider doing an allowance. (There are pros and cons to this, you decide). Giving an allowance mimics adulthood in a powerful way -- you work, you get paid. This only really works if you do make it a consequence rather than a reward. Don't go into it with "you'll get your allowance IF you do your work," but rather, "you'll get your allowance WHEN you do your work."

If you'll have a "when" attitude rather than an "if" attitude, it will teach your child to see the positive consequences of her behavior, rather than viewing the outcome as an optional reward that she may choose to forego some days.

Finally, Focus on the Benefits of Growing Up

Yes, there is some drudgery to adulthood, but growing up is awesome in a lot of ways. Let's face it, you can choose to eat ice cream before dinner if you want, and no one can stop you!

So when your child is struggling with some added responsibility of growing up, work with him to see the advantages of getting older, and how those actually outweigh the additional responsibilities.

No, I'm not going to come in every morning and make sure you're awake and fix your lunch for you before school. *But*, you're old enough to have your own cell phone where you can set a pleasant-sounding alarm, and you can (within reason!) make your own choices about what you want to put in your lunchbox.

If you've followed the first two steps and started early with small responsibilities, and tied in positive consequences, you child will have an even easier time seeing how the benefits of growing up outweigh the additional burdens.

KidsPartyCharacters.com Can Help!

One good way to motivate your child to keep up with her responsibilities is to focus on future events. Who wouldn't want to have a clean room to show Princess Ariel when she shows up at your birthday party? Or a dog poop-free backyard so you can play tag at your party with Captain America?

Again, focus not on the character coming to your child's party as a reward, but just talk about how your child will want to present herself and her space when her favorite character is around.

Browse our collection of over 200 popular characters now at kidspartycharacters.com and motivate your child into action by booking her favorite character for her next party. We have packages to fit any party, including multiple characters, face painting and balloon artists.

Connect with us on [Facebook](#) for ideas, inspirations, and success stories from other parties.

Parenting tips and More

These amazing parenting tips that are on my blog, can also be useful tools for dealing with parties and your new business.

Parenting Tip: How to Raise an Entrepreneur

If someone were to ask you what you'd like your child to be, words such as kind, honest, and happy might come to mind.

Most of us would be uncomfortable pegging a career for our kids, we want them to be what they want to be (with a few restrictions of course!)

And what's the use really, chances are if we tried to dictate our child's career path she'd likely purposefully go in the opposite direction, anyway.

So, before we talk about how to raise an entrepreneur, perhaps the better question is why would I want to raise my child to be an entrepreneur?

After all, it doesn't take much experience as an entrepreneur to know that it can be a difficult and uncertain career path, and is sometimes simply a code word for "I'm unemployed."

Even if you have no desire to try to put your child on a certain career path, there are at least two reasons you should raise her to be an entrepreneur.

First, we live in uncertain and changing economic times.

It used to be common for people to get a job straight out of college and retire from that same company.

Such stability among jobs and companies themselves is rare anymore.

Equipping your child to be an entrepreneur is a good plan even though she may end up there someday out of necessity rather than choice.

Second, if you raise your child to look at the world through the eyes of an entrepreneur, you're empowering her to know she doesn't have to settle for a life that's lived around a job she hates going to every day, or a boss or co-worker she can't stand.

You're breaking open the traditional model of get the best job you can and stay there for the money whether you like it or not because that's life and giving your child brighter paths to consider.

So, without having any expectation that your child *should* actually become an entrepreneur, let's look at four areas in which you can instill the entrepreneurial spirit in her that will benefit her no matter what profession or job she ultimately chooses.

Discipline

How we discipline our children has a big influence over their self-image and self-esteem.

If we want to raise strong, self-assured, independent children, then we have to focus on problem solving rather than punishment as a method of discipline.

Ruling with an iron hand that metes out punishments in exchange for wrong doing sends your child the message that something's wrong with him.

It also sets the tone for a future boss/employee relationship where your child as the employee simply takes what the boss doles out and lives for Friday night where he can sit at the bar with his co-workers and bad mouth the offending boss.

If your child's wrong doings are met with the attitude of "you have a problem, how can I help you solve it and get your behavior on track?" it helps to build your child up rather than tear him down.

Positive discipline instills ever-important problem-solving skills in your child and empowers him to grow, rather than just leaving him angry with you and questioning his own worth.

One of your biggest roles as a parent is arming your child with a positive self-image because self-image is one of the best determiners for whether he will go on to live a happy and successful life.

Keep this fact in mind when making choices on how to discipline your child.

Money Management

As soon as you feel your child is ready, start teaching her money management skills with small amounts of her own money.

In these early stages, you'll have some say over what she does with her own money so that she grows up with good money habits.

This is a big issue for entrepreneurs because there is no "steady paycheck," especially in the beginning.

As an entrepreneur you have to know how to save for the lean times, the value of reinvesting in your business, and the reality of having to set some of your earnings aside for taxes.

You can teach your child this by at first mandating that she can only spend a certain portion of the money she receives.

Then help her decide what the rest needs to be set aside for.

There may be a portion for saving up for big items she wants, or for extra spending money during a planned vacation, a portion for unexpected things that come up that she may want to participate in or buy, and a portion for the favorite charity of her choosing.

If you'll force this early attitude of not spending everything she gets, it will become a habit that follows her for life and allows her to make wise financial decisions, even if she does wind up with a steady paycheck.

Goal Setting

One of the cornerstones of entrepreneurial success is goal setting.

If you don't define clearly what you want, your chances of getting it plummet dramatically.

All of the research surrounding goal setting shows that people who clearly define their goals, write them down, and share them with someone have a dramatically increased chance of actually meeting their goals.

So why not start early teaching your kids the best and easiest way to get what they want?

Again, it's about instilling good habits that will serve your child for life.

Let your child choose his goals, although you can help by suggesting things that are important but might not be at the top of his list.

The goals could have to do with saving for a big purchase, getting a certain grade, improving a sports performance, making up with a friend . . . what they are isn't nearly as important as writing them down and developing a plan to reach them is.

Growth Mindset

If you haven't read Carol Dweck's book Mindset, it's a must-read for entrepreneurs and parents.

Dr. Dweck's framework states that people either have a growth or fixed mindset.

Those with a fixed mindset believe that their abilities, talents, and intelligence are fixed or determined traits.

Those with a growth mindset know that they can get smarter, develop more abilities, and grow their talents through putting in time and effort, basically doing the work.

For entrepreneurs, growth mindset is an essential trait, one you can't live without.

How do we encourage a growth mindset in our children?

First of course, by modeling it in ourselves and showing our children how our abilities and talents are continuously growing.

As for your child, you'll have to instill in him through your words and actions that there's enough in life for everyone, that the world is an abundant place.

Encourage him to explore different things to discover what his passions are, and allow him to change directions, in fact encourage it.

As a society, we ask kids what they want to be from the time they're preschoolers, and then force them to choose a path when they begin college at 18 or 19 years old ~ a crucial time when they haven't even figured out who they are yet.

Letting your child know that there is no end to the journey, and that changing paths is always okay, sets him up for a lifetime of happiness being who he wants to be and embracing the fact that it may change over the years.

Feed Your Entrepreneurial Spirit at Kids Party Characters

At Kids Party Characters, we've got both you and your child covered.

Help feed your child's imagination and love for life by booking her next party though KidsPartyCharacters.com.

We have over 200 characters to choose from, each of whom is portrayed by trained actors who put on a show for your child and her guests that is guaranteed to create lasting memories.

We also have available all your child's favorite party activities such as face painting, balloon twisting, and cotton candy.

For mom, we have a unique opportunity to have your very own Kids Party Characters business.

With a license to KidsPartyCharacters.com you'll have an exclusive territory in which to book parties, the right to use all of our 200+ costumes, access to our casting director and acting coach, and business training and support from Kids Party Characters founder Cheryl Jacobs.

If you're a stay at home mom looking for an opportunity to work from home, or an entrepreneur looking to add another income stream, book a call with Cheryl right here and she'll answer all your questions and determine whether this is the right opportunity for you.

And don't forget to connect with Kids Party Characters on Facebook, where you'll find daily updates on all the fun we create at children's parties, as well as strategies for growing a business while raising happy and healthy kids.

Teaching Children about Safety

EXPECIALLY AT CHILDREN'S PARTIES

Since you are still reading this eBook I am sure you are getting ready to make your decision to join Kid's Party Characters as a franchise owner, so you need to know as much as possible about kids and safety since you will be entertaining them in many locales both indoors and outdoors.

Having children that are old enough to take care of themselves is at the same time a big relief and a source of great stress.

Yes, it frees up a lot of time when your child is able to walk to school or the store or a friend's house by herself and you get to retire from being a full time taxi driver.

But, especially at first, we often find ourselves as moms spending that extra time worrying about whether they got there or looking at our phones wondering why they haven't texted us yet.

To make things even trickier, we don't want our kids to live in fear.

On the one hand, we need them to know there are bad people out there who might try to hurt you or take you.

On the other hand, we don't want them to walk around in fear all the time, wondering if it's going to happen to them today.

The sad reality of the day is, we have to explain a little more of the real world to them than we want to.

At What Age Should I Have "The Talk" With My Child?

Again, it's going to have to happen earlier than we want it to.

When your child starts doing anything without you, she needs to be prepared for an ill-intended adult to come along.

So, if you're dropping her off at the mall with friends, if she's walking anywhere alone, if she's staying home alone, it's time to have a safety talk.

How to Prepare Your Child Without Scaring Him

This is the hardest part, how to give the right information without saying too much, in a way that he'll know it's serious but not have nightmares or anxiety over it.

Start by explaining to your child that millions of kids walk around alone all day every day and never have a bad experience.

Tell him chances are great that he'll go through life without encountering an adult who wants to hurt him in any way.

But, tell him that because even the small possibility of it happening is so serious, you want to prepare him for it because kids who are prepared for the worst have the best outcome.

In other words, if he's prepared for it, the chances of someone successfully taking him or hurting him in some way go down even further.

Explain to him that just like you prepare at school with fire and intruder drills, (and hopefully you've never had the real thing at your school!), you're going to prepare for rare but scary possibilities in life outside of school.

When he knows this is simply a way to keep him safe, and not a sign that he's going to be placed in an unsafe situation, hopefully it will reduce the tension around the subject.

What to Say to Your Child to Keep Her Safe

You may think some of this is obvious, but your child needs to hear it, even if her response is a bored look and an, "I know mom!"

As humans, when we're in a stressful situation sometimes our common sense can freeze up.

So make sure even the most obvious is drilled into your children so their reactions will be automatic.

Teach your child her name, address, and phone number as soon as she's able to remember it.

1. When She's Home Alone

Keep the doors locked and don't answer them when you're home alone.

If someone comes to the door, just move away from any window or point of visibility and wait for them to leave.

If they are trying to talk to you through the door, do not respond and do not believe any reason they may try to give you for coming to the door.

If you feel threatened or scared at any time, call me.

If someone is ever trying to turn the knob or get into the house in any way, dial 9-1-1 immediately.

2. When She's Walking Alone

As a parent, you need to think about what you want to equip your child with while walking.

Some kids/parents may feel most comfortable if their child has a key ring with a whistle attached to it.

Most kids have cell phones at a very young age these days, and even if you see the lack of necessity there, you may want to get your child a simple flip phone (doesn't have to be a smart phone) so she can call you if she ever feels uncomfortable, or 9-1-1 if she thinks she's in danger.

Here's what you'll want to tell her about walking alone:

Avoid walking alone whenever you can. Try to walk as far as possible with a friend, or even just in sight of another child or group of people you don't know.

When you are walking alone, avoid shortcuts and stay on main, well-traveled streets as much as possible.

Never approach a car that stops and asks you anything.

If you can answer the question from where you are, quickly do so and move on. Don't engage in conversation with someone in a car. Tell the person you need to go and keep walking.

If someone ever tries to touch you or grab you, scream as loud as you possibly can. Kick, fight, make the most commotion possible, no matter what they're telling you.

Noise draws attention and is the number one way you'll escape a potential abductor.

Don't be afraid of feeling like a "baby." If you're uncomfortable for any reason, call me or a friend and we'll talk you to your destination.

3. When She's Anywhere Without a Responsible Adult

Again, as the parent, stress the "don't go down without a fight" mentality.

If someone tries to grab you, keep screaming, yelling, resisting, and fighting, no matter what the person is saying to you.

Run or move towards the most populated or public place there is if you feel in danger or actually are.

For younger kids, if you get lost in a mall or similar setting, seek out the closest store clerk and ask for help. Stay put until your parent or adult is found.

Don't assume just any stranger will help when you're lost, most will, but you have a guarantee you won't get abducted or hurt by a store clerk who's at her job.

Never be afraid to call me because you think I'll be mad at you.

Even if you're someplace you shouldn't be, doing something you don't have permission to do, or with someone you shouldn't be with, if you feel uncomfortable, call me.

Your safety is my number one concern and we'll sort out any wrongdoing on your part after you're safe.

"Better safe than sorry" is a worn-out phrase because it's true.

It's better to sound a false alarm than to get in a troublesome situation that could have been avoided by running away, screaming, or making a phone call.

Parenting Tips for Keeping Children Safe at Home and at Parties

One of the biggest things you can do to keep your children safe is establish open and trusting lines of communication from an early age.

This ensures your child won't hesitate to contact you when he feels unsafe.

It also reduces the risk of your child becoming the victim of a predator who may stalk your child and try to gain his trust over time for unsavory reasons.

Pay attention to what your child does and take notice of any adults who seem to be paying special attention to your child or who are popping up in your child's life repeatedly without specific cause.

If open communication is established, your child is more likely to tell you if an adult is making him uncomfortable.

Stress to your child to always tell you if another adult asks him to keep a secret or not tell you about something.

Reassure your child that it's okay to be rude to any adult that's making him feel uncomfortable.

Monitor your child's internet usage, and keep computers in central, well-traveled locations in the house.

As your child gets a little older, consider having him take a safety course at a local martial arts studio. Most places offer a special one-time or series of classes specifically designed to teach children (and adults) simple but effective moves for getting away from would-be abductors.

End on a Positive Note

Making these conversations serious but not scary can be the trickiest part of it.

End by reassuring your child that we all know a lot of things we never have to use and you're sure this will be one of those things for her.

Let her know that just having conversations about safety goes a long ways towards making her safer and that's why you do it.

Answer her questions and fears truthfully, but without giving more information than needed for her age.

Bring up some good memories and fun, safe times she's had if you have a child who has some anxiety around this topic.

And of course, here at Kids Party Characters, we're happy to help you when the time comes to create those fun memories.

Book your child's next party at KidsPartyCharacters.com and your child will have over 200 characters to choose from as her special party guest.

Her character will put on a fun and interactive show for your child and her guests, and we'll bring along all the extras like face painting, balloon twisting, and cotton candy if you'd like.

For more tips on raising happy and healthy kids, as well as updates on all the magic we create at Kids Party Characters, connect with us on Facebook for daily updates.

Healthy Snacks and Party Food Ideas

GREAT PARTY CONVERSATION

For many parents, one of the biggest joys of having the kids go back to school is that they aren't raiding the pantry or refrigerator once an hour looking for a snack.

It's amazing how long they can go at school without a bite to eat, yet teeter on the edge of starvation if they miss their hourly feeding at home.

The downside to not eating much at school is of course that they come home hungry.

And even if you are there to greet them, you usually don't have the time or desire to put together the dinner before dinner they're requesting.

Rather than having them throw a frozen something in the microwave, try out these healthy snacks that come recommended from some of our kids here at Kids Party Characters.

We've included snacks that many kids will be able to make themselves, some no-bake options that you (or even the older kids) can quickly throw together, and a few choices that take a little more time but are definitely worth the effort when your hungry angel walks in the door after a long day at school.

DIY Snacks

Chocolate-Dipped Oranges: Peel some clementines or regular oranges, melt some bittersweet chocolate, dip the oranges in the chocolate and then sprinkle a little coarse sea salt over the chocolate.

Celery with peanut butter: A traditional favorite that involves nothing more than cutting up some celery and putting peanut butter down the middle.

You can also stick some grapes along the peanut butter (creating a snack younger kids have fun with since they look like "caterpillars.") Pieces of apple stuck in the peanut butter is another option kids like.

Apple sandwiches: Core an apple and then cut it horizontally into thin slices. The apple slices then become the bread for your sandwich.

You can start with a base of peanut butter and stick whatever you want onto the peanut butter -- raisins, coconut, dried fruit, chocolate chips . . . top it off with another slice of apple and you have a unique and tasty sandwich.

Peanut butter pretzel sandwiches: Create your sandwich by spreading peanut butter between two pretzels. Then dip the pretzel sandwich in chocolate and you have a great sweet and salty treat.

Smoothie: You can make these ahead or teach the older kids how to do it themselves. The nice thing about smoothies is you can make up any recipe you want.

Generally, you'll want to start with a base of one cup of some type of milk (cow, almond, coconut, soy), add a few ice cubes, 4-8 ounces of yogurt, and a big handful of your favorite frozen fruit.

You can use juice instead of yogurt, but it spikes the sugar content awfully high.

You can always throw a banana in, even if your child doesn't like to eat bananas, as the taste is consumed by the other fruits.

Smoothies are also a great place to add additional nutrition without spoiling the taste. You can add a teaspoon or two of flaxseed meal or oil, nutritional yeast, protein powder, or chia seeds (if your child's okay with the texture of those).

Mini Pizzas: If your kids need a hearty snack, this is a great one they can make themselves. You'll just need to keep on hand some mini pizza shells, a jar of pizza sauce, and your favorite kinds of pizza cheese and toppings.

They'll have fun creating their own little pizza, it cooks in just a few minutes in the oven, and there's little mess or cleanup.

Frozen yogurt grapes: Freeze some grapes, put a toothpick in each frozen grape, dip them in yogurt and return them to the freezer (for a minute or all day if you're making them in advance).

You can also dip the yogurt-covered grape in other toppings before freezing it if you want. Coconut or crushed nuts add texture that many kids like.

Graham Cracker Fruit Pizzas: Spread a thin layer of cream cheese on a graham cracker and then add your favorite fruit into the cream cheese for a pizza that's ready to eat.

This works great with freshly cut in-season fruits, but you can also use frozen fruits.

No-Bake Options for Adults and Older Kids to Prepare

These will take a little more preparation just because they have a few more ingredients, but they're still simple and provide a heartier option than some of the snacks kids can make themselves.

Simply click on the name of the snack and it will take you to the recipe.

[No-Bake Granola Bar Bites](): These use honey instead of sugar, and the recipe can easily be doubled or tripled so you'll have extras to store in the freezer.

[No-Bake Chocolate Banana Energy Balls](): If you have a couple of ripe bananas, this is the recipe for you. Within the recipe there are also links to a couple of tasty variations on this recipe. The recipe calls for Truvia, but you can substitute honey or the sweetener of your choice.

Steel Cut Oatmeal Energy Bites: This is a great variation on the no-bake options because it uses steel cut oats, which are healthier and have a unique texture that kids often like.

No Bake PB&J Energy Bites: If your child finds the traditional PB&J too boring, give these a try for something a little different and even a little healthier.

For When You Have a Little Time

None of these options will keep you in the kitchen all day, but they do require baking and have a few more ingredients than the other snacks.

They are however kid favorites and may even be good projects if you have an older child who's expressed a real interest in baking.

Double Chocolate Peanut Butter Muffins: The name pretty much says it all here, how could you go wrong with these?! But don't be afraid that they sound too good to be healthy, you'll be surprised to find the focus on good-for-you ingredients and your kids won't even miss all the sugar.

PB&J Bites: If your kids like the no-bake version above, they'll probably like this one too. And if they don't go for the no-bake version, give these a try, they use real jelly and are different enough from the no-bake variety to appeal to kids who want you to actually cook them something!

Zucchini Chocolate Chip Mini Muffins: This recipe has a little longer ingredient list, but it's worth the effort. Don't tell your kids you're feeding them zucchini and they'll never know.

Bonus Pick

So many families are gluten free these days, that it's worth including this recipe for gluten-free, vegan goldfish. These are surprisingly good and can obviously be made in any shape if you don't have a goldfish cookie cutter lying around.

The author of this recipe actually took the time to create a mouth and eye on each goldfish, but I promise you can skip this step without sacrificing the taste and without being considered a bad mom!

This goldfish recipe is a really good option to have around at parties too, just to make sure all guests feel included even if they have dietary restrictions.

In fact, all of the snacks we've included here would provide fun and tasty finger food options at your child's next party.

Parent Tips: Balancing Work and Life

TO SUCCEED IN THIS BUSINESS

Maintaining a work-life balance is especially important if you're a stay at home mom. There's a lot of controversy about whether work-life balance is something *anyone* should strive for because it can be impossible to separate work from life. Constantly striving to balance the two, some argue, just creates unnecessary stress as you work towards a futile goal.

But as stay at moms (and dads!) finding a balance is crucial because you'll have to work from home. This means that the normal physical barriers that provide a forced separation between work and life are absent. The risk of imbalance then becomes greater.

Fortunately, if you'll put some rules in place, it will take the stress out of the process and lead to a much happier home for your kids and family. Following these simple rules will also make achieving work-life balance a very doable goal.

As a stay at home mom, the first thing you have to consider is what you want the "work" side of your life to look like. Let's face it, when the "life" side of life involves being responsible for raising children, there's already a lot of work involved.

The first question to ask yourself then is, do I want to add work, outside of raising children and all the responsibilities that comes with that, to the equation? In the beginning, many moms answer "no" to this question, happy to let their children and household responsibilities define work for them.

As the months, or even years, go on however, many moms have a longing to have something more, something of their own. As one mom put it, "I want to be more than the person that drives the kids to soccer every day."

Financial considerations, especially when raising active kids, also often make this decision for us, forcing us to pick up some paying work to give our kids the lifestyle we want them to have.

If this is you, and you long to (or need to!) have a work identity outside of "mom," then there are three "rules" of sort that will keep you, your family, and your work, happy and balanced.

1. **Establish a Work Zone and a Schedule**

You don't have to have an office to make working from home doable. But you do need some clearly defined boundaries. Your children should know that if mom's in this chair, or this corner, or at this space, she's working and isn't available.

In addition to this "forbidden zone" you need a schedule. You can't expect your kids to not need or want you anytime you wander into your work space. (Although there certainly is something appealing about being able to escape like that on some days, isn't there?!)

Your schedule doesn't have to be consistent every day or every week, but you should make up a weekly schedule and have it posted somewhere that your kids can see it.

2. **Know Where Your "No" Line Is**

The thing about most every kind of work is that it will take up as much space as you give it. So you'll need to establish a firm stopping point. This could be a number of hours a day or a week you'll work. And to **anything** that comes up after that, you say "no" to it, without hesitation or exception.

This may include not working after a certain time at night, not working on the weekends, or not allowing for interruptions during specific family times.

Even though you already have a schedule and a designated work zone, things will pop up when you are on your off hours. Knowing specifically when you'll say "no" to these things keeps you from being tempted to do "just one more thing" and keeps your family from being disappointed when you end up working during family time.

3. Incorporate Your Children Into Your Business

Your children will be happier, as will you, if they can be a part of this thing with you. As they get older, they can take on more and more responsibilities for you. They can do things that make them feel like they are helping of course, but you'll be surprised by how many things they can do that actually ARE a big help.

Talk to your kids about responsibilities they'd like to take on to help you out. When they're younger, they can start out cleaning your work space. They can work their way up to helping you with small office tasks, organizing, checking supplies, helping to keep your calendar, and even doing some customer service help as they get older.

This is a great way to teach your kids responsibility, to make them happy that you're working and not available to them 24/7, and to help you get more done. As an added bonus, you can even pay your kids, have them pay for some of their own expenses, and reap the benefits of having them as your salaried worker when it comes to tax time. Talk to your accountant about this one, it can really save you money.

What does this mean for you? As a licensed member of kidspartycharacters.com, you get an exclusive territory to book appointments, the right to use all of the company's costumes, access to a casting director who will hire and train the character actors, and ongoing support from me.

This is one business your kids would certainly love to be involved in, and it gives you the flexibility of working as many, or as few, hours as you choose. Read more about this fun and profitable opportunity on our website. We're excited to talk with you about the possibilities!

Parenting Tips: 10 Game IDEAS

SOME GREAT PARTY IDEAS

One of the universal constants in life is the exasperated, whiny, "Are we there yet?" that inevitably comes from the backseat for any car ride over an hour.

Built-in DVD players, hand-held gaming systems, and iPads have given some parents a bit of relief from this question.

But even those get old after a few hours. And really, do you want your child lost in his own world staring at a screen?

No, you don't. First, there's all kind of research about how bad this is for him.

And second, common sense just tells us that interacting and having fun with family is a healthier option.

So instead of dreading that road trip that comes along with your summer vacation, look at it as more time for some quality family bonding.

In addition to the standard favorites you should pull out like war, tic-tac-toe, and hangman, here are 10 games you can play to erase the boredom and increase the fun of being stuck in the car.

License Plate Game

Print a map and bring along some crayons and color in each state when you spot a license plate from that state.

This is a great geography lesson and can also be turned into a competition for older kids by having each child (or team of children) take different sides of the road.

If you want to be really fancy, Melissa & Doug makes a [wooden board version of this game](#) that allows you to flip a plate over on each state as you spot them.

You can also read the state's motto on the license plate and discuss anything it might tell you about the state.

I'm Going on a Picnic

In this memory game, the first person starts with "I'm going on a picnic and I'm bringing an apple," or anything starting with the letter A.

The next person has the letter B, but also has to repeat the item that was an A. For example, "I''m going on a picnic and I'm bringing an apple and a banana."

Continue through the alphabet, with players being out when they forget a previous item.

This is also a fun learning tool for younger kids, and you can give them hints along the way when they forget words.

20 Questions

One person decides on a person, place, or thing in his mind. You can narrow it down more and say it has to be an animal, or something found in nature, or any category you want.

The rest of the car asks questions to try to figure out what the person is thinking.Does it have fur? Can it be a pet? Does it live in water? Are example questions.

The person who guesses what the animal was, then gets to come up with the next animal.

Restaurant Race

Each person picks a popular restaurant such as McDonald's, Wendy's, or Applebee's.

Each time she sees that restaurant on a billboard, roadside exit sign, or the actual building, she gets one point.

Pick how long you want the game to go, say 20 points for example, and the first person who gets 20 points wins.

Alphabet Game

The goal is to find each letter of the alphabet, in order, on a billboard or other road sign.

This can be a group effort for younger kids, or you can divide into teams with each team taking a different side of the road and see who can get through the alphabet first.

Fortunately-Unfortunately

This is a great game for tapping into your children's creativity.

The first person might say, "Unfortunately, there was a tiger standing by my bed this morning."

The next person has to do a "fortunately" statement, such as, "Fortunately he was sleeping."

The game continues with no rules about the statements needing to be true or possible.

"Unfortunately, my brother woke him up," "Fortunately, I had my tiger tranquilizer gun under my pillow."

The sillier your children get, the more fun the game will become.

Treasure Bottle

This is a fun activity if you have a little prep time before you go.

Fill empty bottles with rice and additional small items such as buttons, paperclips, M&Ms, anything that can get hidden in the rice when you shake up the bottle.

Keep a list of what's in each bottle.

Have your child try to locate and write down (or you keep track of) each item he's found.

It can be just for fun, or a competition to see who can find all of their items first.

Find 50

Each person picks a common item and makes a mark each time he sees that item as you're driving. The first person to get to 50 with their item wins.

The item could be something specific like a flag, creek, or barn, or more general like something red, or a sign containing a specific word.

Would You Rather

One person acts as the questioner and poses two options to the other participants.

"Would you rather go without food or an internet connection for a week?"

The questions can be serious or silly, and often evolve into a conversation about why one choice is better than the other.

Kids really enjoy making these questions up, or you can simply google "would you rather questions" and get hundreds of examples to work from.

My Cows

When someone spots cows, they quickly count however many they see and claim them as "my cows."

When you pass a church, the first person to spot the church says, "I marry my cows." The cows then presumably procreate, and your 12 cows become 24.

When you pass a cemetery, graveyard, or funeral home, the first person to see it says, "I kill your cows," and kills off another player's cows, forcing him to start again at zero.

When you pass a barn, you can say, "I put my cows in that barn," which means they are safe and no one can kill them. It also means you can't marry your cows. After you put them in a barn, you can take them out of the barn when you see another barn.

You can play for the whole trip, or for a specific time period. The person with the most cows in the end is the winner.

There are several variations of this game, including using different animals. You establish whatever car rules you want to make it most fun for your age range.

Expect Some Resistance

Kids often start out grumpy when being forced to sit next to their "gross" siblings for a long period of time.

They may consider your games dumb or boring. Encourage them to just give it a try and they'll surprise themselves with how much fun they're having.

You may need to start off as the leader and a heavy participant in the game, but chances are they'll continue on their own once their mood had lightened a little.

At Kids Party Characters, we obviously love the land of make believe.

We have over 200 characters waiting to show up at your child's next party, which means we've covered just about every princess, pirate, and superhero your child could imagine, and more.

Every child loves characters, whether it's dressing up and pretending they're a certain character, or having the opportunity to meet their favorite character in real life and actually play with her.

One of the great things about characters is that they bring your child's imagination to life.

They give her unlimited opportunities for creative play around different characters, the qualities they possess, and the lives they lead in the land of make believe.

But with so much focus on education these days, from preschools that brag about having rigorous academic training, to "My Baby Can Read" programs that can seemingly have your baby reading before she can talk, a parent can't help but wonder how much time should be spent in the land of make believe.

The good news is, the evidence shows that pretend play in the land of make believe is actually crucial to your child's early learning and life-long development.

To put it simply, *play* should be the young child's version of academic learning.

Today we'll look at some of the reasons why.

Pretend Play Helps Develop Executive Functioning

Executive functioning in the brain is responsible for tasks like self-regulation, planning, organizing and achieving goals.

Strong executive functioning is obviously desirable no matter what stage you're in or what you decide to do with your life.

Several researchers have studied the correlation between pretend play and development of executive functioning in preschool aged children.

While it's hard to establish a solid causal relationship between the two, the studies overwhelming show a correlation between executive functioning ability and the level of pretend play a child engages in.

For example, one study showed that a child's ability to see objects as having various pretend functions, such as a block being used for building or as a pretend piece of pizza in a play kitchen, was highly predictive of the child's executive function abilities.

Another five-week study did show a direct causal relationship between fantastical pretend play and development of executive function.

Here the children who were exposed to pretend play intervention showed improvement in their executive functioning, while those in the control group and those given non-imaginative play intervention showed no executive functioning improvement.

If that's all a little too scientific for you, just go with this takeaway — pretend play enhances development of skills such as memory, focus, self-regulation, persistence in the face of failure, and management of long-term projects.

Pretend Play Develops Your Child's Social and Emotional Skills

When you watch children playing imaginatively together, you'll notice how much communication goes on among them to live out the story.

Pretend play helps your child develop language and communication simply because they're constantly engaged in both while playing.

Pretend play also helps your child develop emotions and empathy for others by walking in another's shoes, and thinking about how it feels to be the person whose role she's playing.

Playing superhero, for example, can teach your child the satisfaction that comes with helping others when she uses her special powers to save the day and defeat the bad guys.

Pretend Play is the Cornerstone of Creativity and Imagination

Pretend play naturally presents your child with an endless number of different scenarios that require her to use logical reasoning and problem solving.

Deciding what or who to be, what game to play, what's needed to play the game, and how the story will all play out taps into the same cognitive skills your child will use in situations throughout her life.

The abstract nature of pretend play also helps your child form memories of how to react to different scenarios and problem solve challenges that come up during his play.

Basically, your child is developing skills for navigating the world as he grows older.

And the more practice he has at this while he's young and not clouded by the way things are "suppose to be" with the world, the more he'll learn to use his imagination and discover creative solutions.

Pretend Play is Easy

Pretend play comes natural to your child, so it's really no surprise that it's your child's first and best teacher.

Encouraging your child to live in the land of make believe is the best thing you can do for him to prepare him for whatever he decides to do with his life as he grows up.

At KidsPartyCharacters.com, we bring the land of make believe to you with characters who are always the life of the party.

We have packages that include all the extras such as face painting, balloon artists, and cotton candy.

To choose the characters and package that are best for you, visit us at KidsPartyCharacters.com, and connect with us on Facebook to learn more about how we can put the magic in your child's next party.

Parenting Tip: Talking about Memorial Day

FOR PATRIOTIC PARTIES

If you ask a child what Memorial Day is about, the most likely answer you'll get is, "That's the day the pool opens."

Research shows that many children are growing up without ever having much understanding of the significance of Memorial Day beyond this highly anticipated first splash in the pool.

A study commissioned by the National WWII Museum revealed that 80% of the adult respondents had only "little" or "some" knowledge of the day and its purpose.

A 2000 Gallup poll showed that only 28% of the people knew the true significance of Memorial Day, that is to honor those who have died in a war. Another 40% believed the day was for remembering and honoring all veterans.

To put your child ahead of most adults, take a few minutes away from the barbecue and beach towels and talk with her about the true meaning of Memorial Day.

Here are a few ideas of how you can approach it to make the discussion meaningful and interesting for your child.

<u>A Day of Gratitude</u>

Talk to your children about this day honoring those who went to work and never came home. Many of them had children just like your kids.

Those we honor on this day won't be home with their kids to eat potato salad and enjoy the summer sun.

A quick online search will reveal personal and specific stories of real people that you can share with your child to help him understand the true impact of losing a loved one to war.

Try not to be a complete downer here, but let's face it, the significance of the holiday is a grim one.

We obviously don't want the kids to sit around crying all day, so approach it from a perspective of gratitude.

Talk about being grateful for all of your child's friends and family members and the fact that they are safe and present at today's celebrations.

Take a few minutes to be grateful for those who served and lost their lives in war.

Do this even if you are a person who does not believe in the conflicts we send our soldiers into.

The politics of war make this an increasingly tough and touchy subject, but remember the purpose of the day, and that the fallen solider didn't choose or maybe even support the battle.

She just showed up to do the job she committed to do in the name of serving her country, and for that we can all be grateful.

What it Takes and Means to Be a Soldier

Whether you'd ever want your child to be in the military, there are many characteristics instilled by military service that are valuable assets for all humans.

Talk with your child about the discipline and commitment it takes to sign up for military service and complete the necessary training to serve in the soldier's area of interest and expertise.

In this sense, military service mirrors other areas of life that require discipline and commitment to be successful.

Another trait of the soldier is courage, as from the moment they sign on, soldiers often go into situations not knowing what to expect and having to trust themselves and learn as they go.

Again, this mirrors civilian life, especially for kids, when trying new and different things can be scary and uncomfortable.

Being a soldier also means learning teamwork, as everyone has their speciality and must learn to work with and rely on other team members to complete any mission.

Teamwork will always take you further than you can go alone in life.

Use this opportunity to talk with your child about the importance of concentrating on his strengths and interests, and not worrying about the things he may not be the best at.

It's impossible, and completely unnecessary, to be good at everything. And if you learn how to work well with others, you'll be more successful just concentrating on what you love anyway.

These are just a few characteristics to get you started. Think about what personally appeals to you and draw the comparison between being a soldier and any aspect of life to share some easy personal development lessons with your child today.

The Beauty of Living in a Free Country

Again this can be a tricky one because there are a variety of beliefs about the purpose of military involvement in different wars these days, but don't let this fact keep you from discussing the beauty of living in a free country with you child.

The very fact that we can openly criticize any and everything our government does is a big advantage of life in the U.S.A. that many children don't even realize since we completely take it for granted.

Talk to your child about the fact that not everyone enjoys the right to free speech, the right to vote, to publicly assemble, and pursue any job or business venture you want.

At some point anyway, these freedoms are all things that had to be fought to gain or keep.

National Moment of Remembrance Act

Possibly in response to the 2000 Gallup poll revealing only 28% of Americans got the true meaning of Memorial Day, Congress passed the National Moment of Remembrance Act that same year.

The Act calls for everyone to take one minute at 3:00 p.m. local time on Memorial Day and stop everything. Use this minute to honor the men and women who have died in service to their country.

Many organizations participate in this minute, including Major League Baseball halting all games for one minute, Amtrak trains blowing their whistles, and bugles across the country playing Taps. If you are driving at the time, turning your headlights on is a common sign of remembrance.

Whatever discussion you decide to have with your child, participating in the National Moment of Remembrance is a nice way to take action on that conversation.

Happy Memorial Day

Despite is sad underpinnings, Memorial Day is a time for celebration and appreciation of life and country, not for mourning death.

At KidsPartyCharacters.com, owner Cheryl Jacobs and all the team wish you and your family a safe and happy Memorial Day, and we can't wait to see you at your child's next party!

Make sure you join us on Facebook to keep up with all that's going on at KidsPartyCharacters.com.

In Closing

This eBook was designed as a simple reference tool for you, if you are considering starting your own Kid's Party Character Company. I have created an exquisite opportunity for you to work directly with me.

Please visit http://www.kidspartycharacters.com to learn more or come find me on Facebook or Instagram.

Let's get you started in the path to financial freedom by setting you up on a Franchise. Own your own company doing something that truly will make you happy.

www.ingramcontent.com/pod-product-compliance
Lightning Source LLC
Chambersburg PA
CBHW030445220526
45464CB00006B/2422